Raising Fen Tigers

An era captured in verse...

By John Taylor

Published by

MELROSE BOOKS

An Imprint of Melrose Press Limited
St Thomas Place, Ely
Cambridgeshire
CB7 4GG, UK
www.melrosebooks.com

FIRST EDITION

Cover designed by Jeremy Kay

ISBN 978 1 906050 06 1

Printed and bound in Great Britain by:
CPI Antony Row, Bumpers Farm,
Chippenham, Wiltshire, SN14 6LH, UK

Thanks to Bruce Frost, Des Smith and The Littleport Society
for their help and support.

CONTENTS

PREFACE

If you live in the Fens or somewhere near,
You'll find these verses interesting to hear.
There are people and places you'll recognise,
You might read about yourself, with surprise.

Don't take offence since there's none meant,
It's just old memories of how it all went.
Depicting the place and mentality of the day,
How it was at school and what we did at play.

Here and there a few names are left out,
In case their descendents are still about.
Don't want to upset anyone or memory tarnish,
But it's said like it was, there's no use of varnish.

Times were not easy for anyone you saw,
It had a lot to do with getting over the war.
But for other people most really did care,
That's why I was glad to grow up there.

If you remember the people and this mentality,
You'll know life was basic, each day a reality.
Chuckle or cry at things we should not hide.
Remembering them all with nostalgic pride.

John Taylor
2007

LITTLE THINGS

The author, his sister Daphne (at the rear) and Janice.

A spit wash in the street,
Sticky and not discreet.
Shiny conkers on strings,
Marbles and other things.

Grey ash from the hearth,
To make a garden path.
Blue socks darned green,
Where a hole had been.

Bread and dripping,
Hot Oxo sipping.
Bubble and squeak,
Leftovers, so to speak.

Loving it when Nan came,
Bringing presents again.
Looking for what she had,
Being called a scallywag.

Nan pouring tea in her saucer,
Being told we didn't oughter.
Matches and cigarettes,
Hidden in her knicker legs.

Black sweets four a penny.
Variety? There wasn't any.
Toffee stuck inside a pocket,
From Mum getting a rocket.

Bubblegum in your hair,
Asking sister if it's still there.
Red tongues from aniseed balls,
Not hearing Mum when she calls.

Spiders in a matchbox,
Frog's spawn to watch.
Cowboys and Indians,
Capturing the little ones.

Scratches, bruises and cuts,
Barbed wire and rusty nuts,
Bows and arrows home-made,
At Sitting Bull we played.

Marvel at many things seen,
Dust in a narrow sunbeam.
Dandelion seeds floating on air,
Having time to stand and stare.

Hurling sticks skyward,
In the Old Churchyard.
Knocking conkers down,
New, shiny and brown.

Grown-ups in the street,
Using words not to repeat.
Policemen big and strong,
With big tall helmets on.

Cold tea with no milk or sugar,
In a Corona bottle tasting bitter.
The corner of fresh bread,
Covered in butter, to us fed.

Scrumped apples tasting better,
Stretching up to post a letter.
Dressing for Sunday School,
A bus to the swimming pool.

Paper aeroplanes that flew,
Having no lace in one shoe.
Whips and spinning tops,
Cat's cradles and lollipops.

Tracing paper and pencils,
Wax crayons and stencils.
Helping Dad bring in the coal,
Licking out Mum's mixing bowl.

On Remembrance Day,
No going out to play.
Church is where most went,
Celebrating lives since spent.

Not understanding why
Old ladies would sit and cry.
Why some men would not go,
Afraid emotions would overflow.

Twelve pennies brown and old
Made a bob, so we were told.
A quarter of sweets
Had to last for weeks.

Little girls with long pigtails,
Washboards and metal pails.
Worms in Mum's mangle,
Getting hair in a tangle.

Riding on a crossbar,
First time in a motor car.
Bicycles with solid tyres,
Bangers and bonfires.

Blowing off in class,
Wanting the smell to last.
Uncontrollable giggling,
Told off for sniggering.

White lies to your mother,
So she wouldn't discover.
Trees there just to climb,
Sweets and sharing mine.

Swirling new spuds in a bucket,
Peeling them, making a racket.
Shelling dad's garden peas,
Our mum, hoping to please.

Being sent to bed early,
Up to mischief quite clearly.
Mum and Dad arguing,
Reasons lost and eluding.

Big sister teasing,
Upset, not pleasing.
Then me doing the same
To little sister over again.

Butterflies and nettle stings,
Remembering special things.
Of precious days gone by,
Lingering, not questioning why.

LITTLEPORT

A quiet village on the edge of the Fen,
Five thousand people lived there then.
This gave rise to the biggest boast,
The largest village from coast to coast.

A place where nothing much would happen,
That's if you ignored the floods in 'forty-seven.
But life in the village could prove you wrong,
As you might know, a lot of little things went on.

The fire brigade at Gas House Green,
With no grass, only gravel to be seen.
The day the Old Granary burnt down,
People from the village gathered around.

The gas works made lots of smoke,
And Mr Constable made tons of coke.
We got excited about some special fun,
When a travelling fair was about to come.

With dodgems and a coconut shy,
And swinging boats that went too high.
There were airguns that fired a cork,
For weeks our fair was all the talk.

People mostly travelled by bus or train,
Hiring Joe Lofts to the station and back again.
The Fenman to London was a sight to be seen,
Hissing into the station through a wall of steam.

Strange accents heard if you were listening,
Men from Sheffield came to do some fishing.
Some folk made a bob by giving them sup,
Praying the taxman wouldn't catch up.

On Saturday mornings we had a treat,
First at the cinema to get a good seat.
Roy Rogers and cartoons in colour for us,
Miss Fisher kicked us out if we made a fuss.

Remembrance Day was for all who care,
The British Legion led this solemn affair.
Every year George Pettit carried the flag.
Around the village we marched feeling sad.

To the library wall we made our way,
For the names of those who died far away.
Then to the church to hear Canon Payne
Speak of their sacrifice all over again.

Ron Barber put on a Soap Box Derby,
Building carts, boys worked like an army.
Martin and me called ours 'Cheetah',
Telling the others, "We are gonna beat ya!"

Making bicycles with no mudguards or lights,
We gathered the bits from many old bikes.
Holding dirt races not far from Camel Drove,
How the slub flew when we got into the grove.

Our mums were masters at recycling clothes,
Sold in the Con. Hall, as everyone knows.
Coming from jumble sales, you understand,
Where our mums would fight, hand to hand.

'Hand-me-down' clothes was a common touch,
I had a big sister, so I didn't care for it much.
If you had clothes that were quite new,
They were always too big until you grew.

Fishing with a jam jar on a string was fun,
Two sticklebacks then home to show Mum.
Away all day, there was an adventure to be had,
Our mums didn't worry about us, or anything bad.

Littleport Show was a special event,
Martin's Field is where we all went.
For sixpence you could bowl for a pig,
Or watch girls at the maypole doing a jig.

Prizes for running all over the place,
Even prizes for a slow bicycle race!
There were prizes for drawing and painting,
Throwing bales over a beam, or just scraping.

Fish and chips for a cheap quick meal,
Eaten from newspaper with great zeal.
Get in line at Snushall's and take your place,
Order your fish, he only ever had cod or plaice.

Shopping would not be the same any more
After Willett opened 'The Walk-Around Store'.
Quite a novelty with the women in our village,
Helping themselves, carrying all they can manage.

From a farm near Hempfield we fetched our milk,
Swinging it over our heads, hoping none gets spilt.
Teachers lived like us, in council houses,
And old Mr Martin pulled carts with horses.

An odd affliction in this big village enclave
Grabbed those who aspired to centre stage.
Especially as chairman of a petty committee,
Grasping importance, getting drunk on authority.

Clearly easy to be a big fish in a small pond,
Didn't understand why others would respond.
It was said that if you asked a simple request,
More authority was in saying 'No' than 'Yes'.

Councillors struggled to behave how they ought,
An authority on everything, or so they thought.
Building a bandstand, even though the band said, "No,"
So we played Davy Crocket there, fighting at the Alamo.

Allotments sometimes provided a surplus,
Quietly given away without reward or fuss.
Kids were no angels and got walloped then,
Those things helped us grow up, back when …

Growing up can seem tough to a little boy. But just when it seems that life is far too hard, a kind word reminds that all is well.

A WORLD OF DON'TS

"Go out and play."
"Come in and stay."
"Sit over there –
come over here."

"Don't you dare!"
"Don't stare."
"Do what you like –
now out of my sight."

"Say *Please.*"
"Don't tease."
"Say *Thank you* –
and use your hankie."

"Don't pout."
"Don't shout."
"Don't be rude –
or get in a mood."

"Don't dirty your clothes."
"Don't pick your nose."
"Don't swing on the gate –
and don't be late."

"Now quickly walk."
"Stop that talk."
"Stay on the path –
    and let others pass."

"Leave your sister alone."
"Wait till I get you home."
"Gonna tell your dad –
    how you've been bad."

"Don't test my will."
"Now just stand still."
"Stop that fidgeting –
    and your scratching."

"Stand up straight."
"Don't call me mate."
"Wear your hat –
    and don't do that!"

"Not on your sleeve."
"No, you can't leave."
"You're not to moan –
    and leave that alone."

"Stand on the mat."
"Don't sit on the cat."
"Don't make a sound –
    and don't you frown."

"Use your fork."
"Leave the stalk."
"Eat your greens –
    as well as your beans."

"Don't bite your nails."
"Stop playing with snails."
"Don't get yourself dirty –
    and be home by 5.30."

"Wash your face
And every other place."
"Then go to bed –
    did you hear what I said?"

"Don't whine."
"It's *that time*."
"Brush your teeth –
    then go to sleep."

"Good night."
"Sleep tight."
"Sweet repose."
"If you fall out of bed,
You'll squash your nose."

LITTLE BOY'S QUESTIONS

Why do dandelions make my hands black?
The sap is white, I don't understand that.
Why do nettles have to sting?
Have I been naughty or something?

Why do sprouts make me stink?
The same reason as beans, I think!
Why do onions make people's breath smell?
When Granddad's had one, you can always tell.

Grown-ups say they want better for us.
But when I ask, just make a fuss!
If I want something I'm told to say 'please'.
But when I do I'm told 'no', is that to tease?

Why is it always too late for ice cream?
Does Milky Way come late to be mean?
Why does my big sister like to tease me?
And then fill her face with looks of glee!

How do birds stay up without flapping their wings?
They must be hanging on invisible strings!
Where do stars go during the day?
Hiding behind the clouds, I dare say.

Why do dogs smell another dog's bum?
I suppose it's their idea of fun.
Why does my dog lick its willy?
It's so rude, and I think he's silly.

Why do grown-ups stop talking when I'm near?
They must be saying things I'm not to hear.
Why does Dad swear and give angry looks?
Then seeing me, he says, "Oops."

Where do babies come from?
She goes red, when I ask my mum!
Why does my dog's back leg twitch?
When I help its spine with an itch.

I try hard not to, but why do I wet the bed?
I'll grow out of it one day, the doctor said.
I yawn when I'm not tired? That's not right.
Worst of all, Mum says, "Early to bed tonight."

HOOKED

Nearly four when my Gran took me to the river,
With a long cane, line and a float of feather.
Garden worms in a jar, fascinating to watch,
To Sandhill Bridge for what we could catch.

Gran toppled as she sat on the grass,
Wouldn't touch a worm, but that did pass.
To me they were just like wriggling strings,
Boys' fingers clearly made for such things.

We didn't wait long before we had a fish on,
I saw red fins while thinking, "It's got no tongue."
A perch with a big mouth and a spiky back fin,
The worm it swallowed had gone deep within.

Gran managed to get our only hook out,
When back in the water it didn't hang about.
It dashed to the bottom, no longer in strife,
But I was hooked for the rest of my life.

Now around the world much I have seen,
Gone fishing in most places that I've been.
Written magazine articles, done radio fishing news,
Littleport is where it all started, on the Great Ouse.

OH DEAR

Oh dear, why do I still wet the bed?
I'll grow out of it one day, Dr Gordon said.

I have tried staying awake all night,
But the Sandman always wins the fight.
Leaving me before it's time to get up,
Then I find I'm still a mucky pup!

If only I could stop wetting the bed,
I'll grow out of it one day, Dr Gordon said.

Allowed nothing to drink after 5 o'clock.
Hoping it will make this awful habit stop.
Try as I might, it's all to no avail,
Every morning it's the same old tale.

Oh why can't I stop wetting the bed?
I'll grow out of it one day, Dr Gordon said.

My mum is going to tell my best friend,
If this watery habit I can't soon mend.
I panic as I am told it is a disgrace,
If she tells him, I can never show my face.

Oh please help me stop wetting the bed,
I'll grow out of it one day, Dr Gordon said.

Desperate to stop, but what a fight,
Waking to check all through the night.
I try so hard not to let it happen again,
But in the morning my heart is full of pain.

Is there magic to stop me wetting the bed?
I'll grow out of it one day, Dr Gordon said.

My mum's patience is long since spent,
She no longer asks how the night went.
Just reaches for the fireside shovel,
And gives my bum it's daily pummel.

I'll run away if I can't stop wetting the bed!
I'll grow out of it one day, Dr Gordon said.

Afraid of sleeping and making a mistake,
Frightened of waking to find what I hate.
But the sheet carries a big yellow stain,
I can already feel the shovel's pain.

I will pray at Sunday school for a dry bed,
I'll grow out of it one day, Dr Gordon said.

I start school in a few short weeks,
Can't go there with sore red cheeks.
What if all the other boys find out?
I'd be teased and shunned without a doubt.

It makes me cry, I can't stop wetting the bed.
I'll grow out of it one day, Dr Gordon said.

But the sun shone bright, one cold, cloudy day,
As I proudly told mum "no sheets to wash today".
I thought she would be as pleased and I wanted to see,
But she frowned and said, "It's about time if you ask me".

Oh joy! I have stopped wetting the bed,
I told you, you would, Dr Gordon said.

Sitting at her desk, Mrs Tabbet had a habit of rocking back on the rear legs of her chair.

AEROPLANES AND CANES

First School Photograph

Up into the sky I liked to stare,
Wondering what went on up there.
"What are all those lines with fluffy tails?"
My dad said, "They are vapor trails."

"What are the 'swirly' ones?" I asked.
"That's dogfighting and going fast."
How dogs could get up there bothered me,
But remember, then I was still only three.

Being fascinated with things that fly,
I wanted to rush around in the sky.
Dad made an aeroplane of wood one day,
It was great, but it could never fly away.

When I was four I started school,
This was an exception to the rule.
They said my birthday was on an odd date,
Otherwise I'd have to start school too late.

Headmistress Davy and her assistant Gill
Ruled school like tyrants, I remember still.
Patrolling the classrooms, stiff and smugly,
Both of them could win prizes for being ugly.

Seeing them coming, you'd give them a mile,
And I never saw either of them with a smile.
They were always together, like Bill and Ben,
Nobody thought anything of it back then.

Our Form Teacher was Mrs Tabbet,
Being nice was her regular habit.
Friday she said, "You can do what you like,
Then we'll all go home, and me on my bike."

Excited, I rolled some paper into tubes,
No time for crayons or building cubes.
I made two tails and some other things,
Then set about making two sets of wings.

But when I launched them into the sky,
No matter what I did they wouldn't fly.
They flopped about and tumbled down,
Until they eventually reached the ground.

At the design centre in a moment of repose,
I decided they needed some weight in the nose.
I looked and I saw, not far from teacher's chair,
Two shiny bolts on the floor, just lying there.

When Mrs Tabbet came to inspect our work,
She saw my aeroplanes and stopped with a jerk.
"Well now, what a clever boy you are,
I'm going to give you your first gold star."

On Monday morning, as was the custom then,
Standing, teacher said, "Good morning, children."
We returned her greeting in a whining droll,
Then we sat down for the register call.

But as she sat down there came a loud crack,
Two legs fell off her chair, still fixed to the back.
She disappeared behind her desk and loudly bellowed,
Two feet appeared, then the rest of her they followed.

Flustered and not knowing what was happening,
She struggled up, telling us kids to stop chattering.
Checking her chair she saw two shiny bolts no more,
She then remembered where she'd seen them before.

Immediately to see Miss Davy I was marched,
Frightened and afraid, my mouth was parched.
I stood looking at the floor without a comment,
Miss Gill towered over me, relishing the moment.

They said I had interfered with the teacher's chair,
Trembling and too afraid to speak … it wasn't fair.
Too terrified to say I'd found those bolts on the floor,
So they caned me hard and made me sore.

I didn't cry … Well, not so they could see,
Boys don't cry. I couldn't let the girls see me.
Mrs Tabbet took me back to class, it wasn't far,
Then she made me remove my only gold star.

Which hurt the most I couldn't say,
Having my gold star taken away,
The stinging cane that made me sore,
Or discovering life when I was four.

INFANTS' SCHOOL TOILETS

In the corner of the old school playground,
Is where the boys' toilets could be found.
There was an open-air trough against a wall,
We peed over it so plants didn't grow there at all.

There were three whitewashed hatches,
Not at all private, they had no latches.
Trying hard not to let any one see you go,
Lest a boy shouts, "Come and see the show."

Old Mrs Fox was an Infant School helper,
One of her jobs was handing out toilet paper.
We were obliged to ask her to give us some.
Two squares was never enough for anyone's bum.

So did we get skid marks? I'll tell you later,
I told my Nan about her meanness with paper.
She said, "Tell Old Mother Fox, her nose I will seek,
Then I'll pull it as long as a wet week."

So I did.

MOTORBIKES AND SPRINKLERS

There were only three cars in our street,
Dad had a motorbike, it ran quite sweet.
But all together he wanted to take us out,
It was quite a problem, without a doubt.

There were five of us, including me,
With my sisters, Janice and Daphne.
Our dad couldn't afford a proper car,
So he built an aluminium sidecar.

When finished it didn't half gleam,
Then he painted it black and cream.
It was a bumpy ride, didn't want to go far,
Had one wheel, Dad didn't keep on the tar.

Excited, to Hunstanton we were to go,
Mum on the back and Dad driving slow.
In the front my sisters would pack,
While I was squashed into the back.

The roof was a black canvas affair,
I'd roll it back to get some fresh air.
If it rained I sucked it through a crack,
Occasionally I was sick out the back.

On our way home, one sunny day,
Cars overtook us along the way,
We'd had a good time and not by half,
The people in cars were having a laugh.

Mum didn't take much notice at first,
Just thinking of tea to quench her thirst,
Then turning around she spotted me,
Standing in the back having a pee.

Chris Lee gave cheap haircuts to men and boys in the evening at his home. My sister was also sent there because he was cheap, she hated it. She was there on this occasion, Mr Lee asked if I had been eating peas. We couldn't stop giggling all the way home and chanted, "Been eating peas at Mr Lee's." Years later, Chris Lee opened a barber's shop at Pont's Hill.

HAIRCUT

When I was little, my grandma came to look after us,
She'd come from London by train and then on a bus.
My mum had gone to Ely to get another one like me,
My dad was not bothered, another one makes three.

We got real excited, my big sister and me,
"Getting a little brother," we said with glee.
But then we were disappointed, which was silly,
The one Mum brought home didn't have a willy.

"That boy needs a haircut," Gran told my dad,
"It's too long and untidy and looks quite bad."
From his pocket Dad gave me a silver tanner,
"Get it cut short so it'll last," in a sullen manner.

So up Friar's Place I went to see Chris Lee,
Past Banyard's house, he liked to wallop me.
Chris Lee cut hair in his washhouse after dinner,
He'd cut hair in the Army, so he wasn't a beginner.

His washhouse was barely seven feet square,
Men and boys stood around the wall in there.
Men a shilling and sixpence for boys like me,
Most men smoked and you could hardly see.

It was packed the night that I went there,
Each taking turn on the one and only chair.
Boys climbed up, sitting on a big square tin,
The sort that biscuits and crisps came in.

While cutting hair Mr Lee sucked on a Woodbine,
The ash fell down my neck most of the time.
"How do you want it?" He would cough and complain.
Didn't matter what you said, it was always the same.

I was ever amazed at how quick he could clip,
And how he never gave your ear a bit of a nip.
Listening to men talk was not very interesting,
All about harvesters and sugar beet singling.

When my turn came Mr Lee lifted me onto the tin.
"Cut it short, so for a while I don't have to come in."
As he clipped I felt a rumble on the tin down under,
It started quietly, and then sounded like thunder.

One man said with great delight,
"Put your fag out, Chris, or you'll go up like dynamite."
"Blimey, that's a waste," another man said,
"You should have saved it to warm your bed."

I sniffed the air, and fell into fits of giggling,
Chris Lee stood back, stopping his clipping.
"Now look here, boy, that's not fair,
I don't have to cut your bloody hair."

From a corner of the room came a cry,
"Oh my God, I think I'm going to die."
Then a tall man left in disgust and little sorrow,
"I won't bother now, Chris – I'll see you tomorrow."

My hair was cut really short, I wondered if for spite.
When I got home my old gran got a terrible fright.
"You look like a convict – my, what a hair cut,
Your ears stick out, so we'll call you 'Wing-Nut'."

As I got older I didn't sit on that big tin any more,
But I got a funny look when I walked in the door.
As Chris Lee's shoulder's dropped he would say,
"I hope you are going to behave yourself today."

It was not unusual to visit the butcher once a week to order fresh meat for delivery during the coming week. Few people had refrigerators. Clearly, at least one butcher, whose name is not mentioned for obvious reasons, made the most of his opportunities.

THE BUTCHER'S DELIVERY

A local butcher, who I won't name,
Had a reputation, or was it fame?
For delivering meat to ladies at home,
Especially when they were all alone.

He'd hand over the meat for his pay,
Then he had something else to say.
Suggestive remarks to try it on,
He tested his charm on my mum.

She was not a woman to muck about,
She punched him hard, right on the snout.
Backwards through the door the butcher flew,
Making a noise that sounded like, "Ooooo."

Through our screen he went with a crash,
Clearly not expecting to get such a bash.
When our dad came home and saw his trellis,
We thought, "I'm thrashing you," he'd tell us!

The butcher woke from where it was black,
He was on our lawn, flat on his back.
Mum told him to stop his mucky ways,
Or she'd tell how he'd woken in a daze.

But she went and told everyone who'd listen,
In our house there'd be no petting or kissing.
What the butcher thought was a likely kitten,
Was a Fen Tiger and he was no longer smitten.

IF YOU WANT TO KNOW THE TIME – ASK A POLICEMAN

Going home was never hard,
Rushing out of our schoolyard.
Although we were taught the crossing code,
A policeman always saw us across the road.

He stood in the middle, on the white line,
Wore great big boots and how they'd shine.
With huge white gloves that reached his elbow,
"Don't you run, you'd better walk slow now."

I asked him, "Can you tell me the time, please?"
He tugged at his glove and pushed up his sleeve.
His glove came off with a disgruntled mumble,
While I stood there trying hard to look humble.

His face went red and his eyes would shine,
When he twisted his arm to check the time.
Sometimes it held up traffic to anguished sighs,
But to those who knew, it was no surprise.

"Half past three," he'd glare and say,
It was the same time every day.
If he saw me coming I didn't have to ask,
Already had his glove off when I went past.

I saw how frustrated he got, every time,
But it was fun for me and I didn't mind.
If only he'd thought to stand the other way,
He could have seen the church clock every day.

FIRST NEW PULLOVER

The author wearing 'the' pullover

Mum decided I needed a new pullover,
I owned but one knitted woolly jumper.
The one I had came from a jumble sale,
A dark green one, washed out and pale.

The wool would be special, one of the few,
Bought from Ginny Webb's and totally new.
Usually it would be recycled from a jumble stall,
Mum would pull it down and wind it into a ball.

Her hands moved so fast it made me stare,
While I held up an old sock, or even a pair.
Watching the stitches as they unwound,
Fascinated as they went round and round.

An ounce each week Mum would buy,
She asked Ginny Webb to put it by.
Over the weeks a dark-red jumper grew,
I was so excited because it was new.

It was finished early one summer eve,
Mum was proud of what she'd achieved.
"Come over here and try it on."
It was not too short and not too long.

Fitting perfectly, I thought I looked a toff,
So I wanted to go out and show it off.
Mum thought to keep it for Sunday best,
So it wouldn't get torn like all the rest.

I begged and pleaded to be let out,
She got frustrated and started to shout.
"Back by seven, take care of that jumper too,
Then a wash, and up the 'Wooden Hill' for you!"

Off to the playing fields I decided to go,
To walk the way round would be too slow.
So I took a shortcut through Brightley's yard.
If you were quick it was not too hard.

It was wrong, there was no pretence,
Up and over that six-foot picket fence.
Across the field to where others played,
If I'd had all night I would have stayed.

I asked the time from someone's dad,
Ten past seven, Mum will be really mad!
Dashing across the field as fast as I could
To that big spiky fence all made of wood.

To the top I climbed, not making a sound,
Didn't want to alert Mr Brightley, I'll be bound.
I should have climbed down facing the other way,
I decided to jump, a mistake that made me pay.

My leap was not far enough from the fence,
Thinking it wouldn't make a lot of difference.
But a picket went up my back to make a hole,
I hung there like I'd been strung up on a pole.

When I wriggled the stitches gave,
I felt they were trying to dig my grave.
Suspended by my pullover on the fence,
Now I was wishing I'd had more sense.

Before long Mr Brightley spotted me,
Clearly in trouble he could plainly see.
So down his garden amused he came,
Then put me back on the ground again.

He told me off for cutting through his yard,
But to keep a straight face he found it hard.
When I got home my mother cried,
For the very first time I wish I had died.

From then on it all happened quite fast,
From my dad I got one hell of a blast.
Off came his belt, no good being meek,
I couldn't sit down for more than a week.

My mother said she would send me away
To a place where naughty boys had to stay.
So I was good, now I mean really very good,
And never went near that tall fence of wood.

RADIO WAVES

Our dad catching radio waves from the sky,
Concentrating on the dial and the magic eye.
Wriggling valves as they were getting warm,
All gathered around, quiet to avoid any scorn.

Wanting a favourite programme to come on,
Such anticipation, it seemed to take so long.
To the lavatory before the programme starts,
You don't want to miss any of the best parts.

Two BBC stations, so there was a choice,
Then from afar would come a posh voice.
We made not a sound to disturb the peace,
Was it my favourite? *Journey into Space*.

Suffering unbearable suspense since last week,
Was it really an alien Lemmy was about to meet?
Will the Captain get free from a poisoned airlock?
Each episode would end at the most exciting spot.

Dad admired Dick Barton and his clever ways,
He'd talk about his exploits for several days.
Mrs Dale's Diary was Mum's daily choice,
Will Dr Jim catch a cold? In a Scottish voice.

The Peter Brough and Archie Andrews Show,
We didn't find it odd ... a ventriloquist on the radio.
The Billy Cotton Band Show was always a hit,
We had Sunday lunch while we listened to it.

Two Way Family Favourites became a ritual,
Listening for names of families that you knew.
Faint scratchy voices with greetings from afar,
From Germany, Cyprus and Kuala Lumpur.

When Vera Lynn sang 'We'll Meet Again'
You could hear Dad's silence and his pain.
Donald Peers would sing a topical song,
Our mum would cheer up and sing along.

Jack Archer told Walter how to plough,
But it was clear Walter already knew how.
Mr Gabriel was a character always doing his duty,
Saying, "Woo – there, me old pal, me old beauty."

One day strange contraptions appeared up high,
On chimneys, catching pictures from the sky.
"It was television," they said, something new,
But it was a long time before we had one too.

We never knew Mr Laws' first name but he was known as 'Rats'. So respectfully for this verse his nickname is used. Mr Laws also owned an antique shop in Crown Lane.

RATS' TUCK SHOP

Rats Laws lived between our schools,
He opened a tuck shop, bending the rules.
Selling gobstoppers and Smith's crisps,
Fruit gums, sherbet and liquorice sticks.

Home-made ice lollies a funny shade of blue,
That left your mouth with a very strange hue.
What they were made of, we dare not think,
But most of us thought it was old school ink.

Old Sharp's toffee that was soft like goo,
If you ate too much you had to go the loo.
But he had to shut down, we never knew why,
So it was over to Dolby's for our goodies to buy.

DOLBY'S SHOP

Opposite the school stood Mr Dolby's shop,
Next to the church in quite a good spot.
He sold groceries, chocolate and sweets,
The things that give your taste buds a treat.

Asking for ration stamps, he heard our sighs,
So we could only go in to feast our eyes.
But when stamps were required no more,
We seldom had money to buy at his store.

Kids are mischievous, that's no surprise,
We went in to check out all his supplies.
Looking for what he didn't have in stock,
Then told him we liked them quite a lot.

"I'll order some in when the traveller I've seen."
So we kept asking for them until he had been.
When the stock came in we changed our mind,
Telling Dolby we liked sweets of some other kind.

It worked with Spangles and Penny Chips,
Going on to torpedoes and barley sugar sticks.
Eventually all Mr Dolby's shelves were filled,
Then when he realised, he could have killed.

Mrs Fitch would often be seen outside her cottage on the pavement, on Wisbech Road, especially at school times. She would wear a flowered-print, double-breasted apron with a tie cord round the middle, carpet slippers and thick, sagging brown stockings. But you mostly noticed her anguished look.

MRS FITCH, GOD BLESS HER HEART

Walking to school every day was slow,
If it was sunny, raining or in the snow.
I couldn't afford to stop and play,
Especially on a windy, rainy day.

During my journey on one wet day,
Mrs Fitch stopped me just to say,
"My Jimmy has forgotten his lunch again,
Please give him this, keep it from the rain."

Going home I could see Mrs Fitch from afar,
Standing on the pavement, her view not to mar.
In her apron and slippers, standing there,
I could just make out her curly grey hair.

A troubled old lady with so many a care,
She waved her walking stick in the air.
As in the distance her Jimmy she could see,
"Come home, Jimmy, it's time for your tea."

"Have you seen my Jimmy at school or play?
He is late home from school again today."
In the direction of school she stared intensely,
To see Jimmy coming would please immensely.

Sometimes I knew what she would say,
So, "Yes, Mrs Fitch, Jimmy is on his way."
I'm sure she knew but couldn't believe,
Her heart played tricks, her mind to deceive.

She'd wait until dark, not wanting to go,
When she went in, she was really slow.
With her old blue eyes cast down,
And on her forehead a sorry frown.

Sometimes she'd go to Miss Lester's shop,
To buy Jimmy a chocolate bar, or some pop.
Slowly, for that was as far as she ever went,
Her old legs were weak and her back was bent.

She would talk about Jimmy and his care,
Ida smiled, as she twisted fingers in her hair.
To humour her with compassion and grace,
And give some extra, to put a smile on her face.

Some kids thought it would be fun
To ask if they could play with her son.
"I don't know where he is," she would say,
"I think he has already gone out to play."

With a worried look, she paused and said,
"I've not seen Jimmy since I made his bed.
If you see him, tell him to come home,
I don't like being here all alone."

I asked my Nan if she knew Mrs Fitch,
"Yes," she said, "I don't see her much.
When we were girls we'd often play,
I thought of her just the other day."

"Did she have a boy?" I asked with reserve,
She paused, as if plucking up her nerve.
"Oh yes," she said. "She had a lovely son,
But he never came home from the Somme."

"Joined the Army, when he was too young,
Afraid to tell his mother what he had done.
They sent him off to fight a war,
Then we didn't see Jimmy no more."

My Nan tried hard not to blink at all,
Lest a tear should accidentally fall.
She said, "I've got something in my eye."
But I could tell she was trying not to cry.

Now Mrs Fitch is in heaven up there,
She will be happy and without a care.
Yes, I believe that's where she's gone,
To be with Jimmy, her beloved son.

Dear Mrs Fitch, I can't forget you,
Nor your brave son I never knew.
That would surprise you now, I bet,
And your dear son. Lest we forget.

Dedicated to Private James William Fitch, First Battalion Cambridgeshire Regiment. Who died on 26th September 1917 … and his loving mother.

DAPHNE'S HAT

Daphne and I went to London by train,
Off to Acton, to see Grandma again.
Mum made Daphne wear a hat she didn't like,
A brown furry thing, it was a terrible sight.

She took it off when we left the station,
Cursing that hat all the way to damnation.
Waiting until the train was travelling fast,
She threw it out the window, gone at last!

"A terrible thing happened," she told our mum,
"We'd put our heads out the window just for fun.
Then a great wind blew it completely off,
Ever so sorry, Mum," she said under a cough.

Sometimes common sense gets lost in petty bureaucracy.

SCHOOL BUS

As an infant I didn't understand some decisions,
Especially when made by people in high positions.
There was no consideration or initiatives to learn,
Just follow the rules, it's not 'your' concern.

Eastwood's bus was hired to give kids a ride
To school and home again, when they were tired.
But who would ride and who would walk?
Was the subject of much debate and talk.

They decided to draw a circle on the map,
If you lived inside you walked, that was that.
With no direct road from my home to school,
First I walked in the opposite direction, like a fool.

In a while I came to where the bus would wait,
Right in front of one lucky student's front gate.
I stood with the others where you get on and off.
The bus arrived, billowing smoke, making us cough.

But a woman refused my entry and made a fuss,
Saying I was not entitled to ride on the school bus.
"Your house is well inside the circle," she cursed,
Not caring how far I'd walked to get there first.

So each day I watched the school bus go by,
With empty seats, I could never understand why.
I'd see that self-righteous woman sitting in the front,
When she saw me, my eyes she would not confront.

My mother saw the teacher for a dispensation,
For me to ride, but it only caused aggravation.
"The rules had been set, which we must follow."
No matter what she said their ears were hollow.

A special friend for many years was Martin Law, his mum and dad were very kind and always considered me.

LEARNING TO SWIM

Martin's dad took us with him
To Sandhill Bridge for a swim.
Martin could swim really good,
Me? I didn't think I ever would.

We came to the huts then went in,
Next to Martin I was painfully thin.
But putting on our swimming trunks,
We thought we were a couple of hunks.

Martin dived in right away,
On the bank I decided to stay.
His dad asked, "Are you coming in?"
So I decided I'd better try to swim.

Into the cold water, doing my best,
I stood there, wet up to my chest.
There I stood until starting to shiver,
In that cold, wet, forbidding old river.

Standing, daring myself to let go,
Something slid over my foot, very slow.
Was it a fish or could it be it an eel?
I lifted my feet and let out a squeal.

Kicking my legs and trying to get out,
Like a windmill, thrashing my arms about.
Suddenly I realised that I did not sink,
Those were my first real strokes, I think.

ECLIPSE

One day at school when I was nearly six,
Mr Cockerel said, "There's to be an eclipse.
The moon will pass in front of the sun."
Ann Cox cried and wanted her mum.

Cockerel lived two doors from my home,
A tall, thin man, all skin and bone.
He wore a flat cap to protect from rain and hail,
It was too big and made him look like a nail.

"Don't look with your naked eyes, you lot."
Funny, I thought, that's the only sort I've got.
"Look through smoked glass or you'll go blind."
So Miss Pollard brought some, that was kind.

We broke it up and each took a piece,
"Now over the candle, if you please."
With more soot on ourselves than the glass,
Covered in black … now what a farce.

I never got to see that cosmic event,
The first aid room is where I went.
To join a long queue, to my surprise,
We all had cuts or soot in our eyes.

GHOST AT NUMBER 29

Uncle Dick

This little boy's home was in Friar's Way,
You'd probably know the house, I dare say.
A council house without much grace,
Guarding the entrance to Friar's Place.

Two up, two down is all it had,
I shared my room, it wasn't bad.
In the back bedroom, my sister and me,
We went to bed early, there was no TV.

Our mum teased us when Milky Way came,
Pretending she was going to give us the cane.
We'd hear her grumbles coming up the stair,
From behind her back, ice creams for us pair.

As we laid there, “What’s that noise?” I said.
“I don’t know, it’s coming from under your bed.”
My big sister made funny noises with glee,
For fun she liked to tease and frighten me.

To our left were two green cupboard doors,
In one our things, we called it ‘mine and yours’.
The other was locked, no idea what was in there,
A big secret, never asking to see, we didn’t dare.

Then one dark night I awoke with a fright,
Through the cupboard door came a scary sight.
A tall, thin man, who at first seemed to have no hair,
Smiling at me, while he appeared to float on air.

Wearing a brown suit, like an all-in-one.
Curly red hair from under the hat he had on.
The front of his helmet saw a name in red,
It was dark, so I couldn’t read what it said.

His ears looked square, or some strange shape,
Down his front hung a tube, like a rubber snake.
He drifted around the foot of my bed,
I dived under the covers to hide my head.

My mum said it must have been a dream,
But to this day I know what I had seen.
We moved to Queen’s Road when I was nine,
The cupboard door was unlocked, it was time.

On the door hung a brown Air Force flying suit,
Leather helmet with earphones built in to boot.
And an oxygen mask with a tube to breathe,
I couldn't stop excitement beginning to seethe.

On the front of the helmet was painted a name,
'R. Farthing' in nail varnish, or much the same.
It was just as I saw it when I was nearly seven,
I got excited and thought, "Oh, what in Heaven?"

My dad said Uncle Dick had given them to him,
To wear on his motorbike to keep warm within.
Mr Farthing was one of Uncle's bomber crew,
Wouldn't mind my dad having them, if he knew.

Six more years before my holiday with Uncle Dick,
I asked about the suit and how he came to have it.
He said, "Bob Farthing had died over there …
We pulled his leg about his curly red hair."

"That suit was thick and very warm like mine,
Wore our masks and helmets most of the time.
Bob had 'bought it', so had no need any more,
I gave it to your dad,… that bloody war."

I'm glad I met Mr Farthing, on that dark night,
Even though he gave me quite a terrible fright.
His story from my uncle was well worth hearing,
Of a tall, brave man with red hair and lots of daring.

The council playing fields were not far from our home in Friar's Way. My sisters and I were often there, but we didn't go anywhere without instructions of some kind.

SWINGS AND ROUNDABOUTS

The author and his sisters

In a field near the church we'd run and shout,
There were swings, slides and a roundabout.
There were things for 'bigguns' and 'littleuns' too.
We had such fun, there was a lot we could do.

The slide was tall and to us very high,
We felt we could almost reach the sky.
It let us see over a corrugated fence,
At apples that would cost at least six pence.

The temptation was great in the Canon's garden,
We scrambled over, without begging his pardon.
But Canon Payne was waiting for us to scrump,
He caught us so easily, I felt like a chump.

He said we were stealing and would tell our dad,
As he took back the apples, every one we had.
Demanding our names and where we live,
Someone else's name is all we would give.

We thought the Canon's hands smelt like feet,
His wife pulled down his old socks ever so neat.
Then with hard work for the one she loves,
She knitted them into pairs of gloves.

Mum gave instructions to my sister and I,
"Never to stand on the swings, or go too high."
What we did with our little sister she never saw,
She'd have thrashed our bums till they were raw.

The amusements could be seen from our landing,
Once Mum saw us on the swings both standing.
Grabbing her bike to come and sort us out,
We were in for it now, without a doubt.

But we were lucky and spotted her coming,
We took a shortcut home, fast and running.
Pushing past our dad who was on the stairs,
Put ourselves to bed, didn't wash, who cares.

KNEES UP, MOTHER BROWN

Knock on her door and head for the street,
Mrs Brown discovers there's nobody to greet,
Full of devilment, laughing and grinning,
"Knees up, Mother Brown," we kept singing.

She chased us both, Francis and me,
To where there was a big solitary tree.
Low branches made it easy to climb,
So we'd shin up there in double time.

Mrs Brown stood breathless beneath the bough,
"You wait, I'll catch you one day," she'd vow.
Loudly singing about the knees of Mrs Brown,
Waiting for her to leave before coming down.

One fateful day we rattled her knocker,
Then with a stick she chased us proper.
Sprinting to our faithful refuge tree,
Oh dear, oh dear – what did we see.

She was laughing, what was wrong?
We stopped singing our usual song.
Handy with a saw was Mr Brown,
He had cut all the low branches down.

At the tree we ground to a stop,
Well, it really was quite a fair cop.
Promising never to do it again,
Lucky not to receive a little pain.

We had thought it all good, clean fun
To upset Mrs Brown and see her run.
But the look in her eyes we had never seen,
And realised that we had been really mean.

With honest regret for what we had done,
We would make it up to her, and some.
Our mischievous ways we would neglect,
Befriending her and showing respect.

TO THE CINEMA WITH DAD

Didn't have TV, like some thereabout,
But now and then my dad took me out.
To the cinema, if a good film was on,
Full of anticipation as we went along.

People would smoke in the cinema then,
And most dashed out before the Anthem.
It was tricky to wait and see the end,
You'd get caught and have to stand.

Dad bought the tickets at a little kiosk,
While Miss Fisher would stand and watch.
Managing the cinema and the crowd,
Ever officious with a voice really loud.

Big earrings and too much makeup on,
Just like a bad advertisement for Avon.
She specially enjoyed telling children off,
Even during the film if you had to cough.

While the film was on she'd spray the air,
With a hand pump, pointing it everywhere.
Thinking she'd rid the stale cigarette smell,
It was equally bad, as everyone could tell.

One night while sitting next to my dad,
The man behind mumbled, "Ooo, that's bad."
Complaining and groaning he moved away,
My dad just sat there with little to say.

Asking, "What's that smell?" But I couldn't say.
Then Miss Fisher came with pump and spray.
Pumping hard she covered Dad that night,
He spluttered and thought it was not right.

As we left, Miss Fisher gave a stare,
Arms folded and glaring as if to dare.
After a couple of weeks we went again,
And got that look, as if she was in pain.

She stepped out and stopped my dad,
Then with that bossy look that she had,
"I hope you will behave yourself this eve,
If you don't I will have to ask you to leave."

To my surprise Dad was struck quite dumb,
Unusual after all the practice he had with Mum.
Puzzled he nodded as we continued in,
Then sitting, waiting for the film to begin.

Before long came that awful smell again,
People moved away starting to complain.
Dad sighed, "What *is* that terrible smell?
Like something's died and gone to hell."

The spraying performance was re-enacted,
But Dad didn't speak, that's how he reacted.
As we left, Miss Fisher looked like thunder,
I smiled at her, trying to soften her dander.

When we got home Dad told my mum
About all the things that had been going on.
I sat and listened agreeing here and there,
As he explained Miss Fisher's terrible glare.

Adding, "Where did that stink come from?
It was awful … the most horrible pong."
I piped up, saying with great authority,
"Don't worry, Dad … it was only me!"

I didn't get taken to the cinema again.

Mr Speed was a strict teacher, but a good one. As a disciplinarian you didn't fool about in his class (unless you were very brave). This is how he came to be called 'Om'. That is who he was known as to all students. The name was not used in a derogatory or disrespectful way. It was simply his nickname.

CHRISTENING OM

The whistle sounded in the old school yard,
It was Mr Speed, red faced, blowing hard.
The kids all ran and jostled to get in line,
Couldn't afford to be last, not this time.

Mr Speed was on playground duty this day,
"Late," better have something good to say.
He was a good teacher but very stern,
He always insisted that you learn.

He heard a noise from within the line,
It was Roger Law, talking this time.
Roger was a playful, cheeky sort,
But this day, he really didn't ought.

Speed loudly demanded, "What's going on?"
Then sarcastically, "Laddie, will it take long?"
"Om doing nothing, Sir," Roger quietly sighed,
"Om – Om. Who is this Om?" Speed replied.

Chanting loud, like a Buddhist monk on steroids,
He boomed out, "Om," poor English to emphasise.
It sounded quite funny to the kids in the line,
They went about chanting, "Om," for some time.

So Mr Speed became known as 'Om',
But never to his face, or you were gone.
He must have known, but it was too late,
The name was sealed to him, like fate.

"Now what were you doing?" he demanded again,
"I was doing nothing, Sir," Roger said without refrain.
"Write me six pages about 'Nothing', if you please."
So Roger gave him six blank pages just for a tease.

You can guess what happened next,
Speed threw the book and all the text.
But the name remained and was passed on and on,
Through years of students who knew Mr Speed as Om.

Once every year the police would conduct a safety inspection of bicycles at schools. If you got a red label you were subject to disciplining from your teacher and it was a source of fun and teasing from other students.

BICYCLE INSPECTION

The police checked bicycles at our school,
Some kids had new bikes, they were cool.
Through the cycle sheds the police inspected,
To see which bikes nasty faults had infected.

If your bike was sound and looking clean,
They would tie on a label, all in green.
If it needed a little adjustment somewhere,
They would tie an orange label right there.

Should your bike be found dangerous in the shed,
You couldn't ride it home and got a label, bright red.
Mustn't take it off, walk home and show your dad.
But that only happened if your bike was really bad.

Two shops did repairs, Bert Dye and Ted Bamber,
Both hoped for lots of labels darker than amber.
When the police inspected, business was abundant,
For much of the year repairs were all but redundant.

When it was over and the police had gone,
We looked at the bikes to see what they had on.
Many were orange and a few there were green,
Those left, the owner's too embarrassed to be seen.

One old red machine stood out from the rest,
I'll try to describe it, and do my level best.
Om not saying which teacher owned that bike,
It rattled and squeaked, and was quite a sight.

You might know who owned that old thing,
It made a noise like a pig trying to sing.
When you saw it, you couldn't help but gaze,
This rickety old racer had seen better days.

Being full of devilment and looking for fun,
We tied red labels to it, with comments on.
That teacher walked home in disbelief,
His bike decked out like a 'Raleigh Chief'.

For weeks he walked to school and home again,
No one dared to tell him, we didn't want the cane.
So we lived in fearful excitement, that was clear,
Until the next time we could bait without fear.

DISCOVERING HYPOCRISY

I borrowed a bike from one of my friends,
Went on an adventure to explore the Fens.
Going a long way to see what was there,
Riding for hours without much care.

Getting a puncture in the front tyre,
A bicycle pump was my only desire.
My friend's bike didn't have one fitted,
It was nice, but not quite fully kitted.

I could see for miles, not a house around,
There were only birds to make a sound.
Then a distant figure came out of the sun,
I needed a pump so I hoped he had one.

An ancient old man appeared on the drove,
He got off his bike to look, but didn't move.
"Please may I borrow your pump?" I asked.
He continued to look, then spoke at last.

Slowly raising his head and then his voice,
Clearly looking for words and making a choice.
He stared at me with his watery blue eyes,
Somehow I knew I was in for a surprise.

He waved his finger and started to rant,
About Biblical maidens and their lamps,
Of being prepared for the Lord to see,
He knew the verses, directing them at me.

Then with low grunts as though in pain,
He started off down the drove again.
I thought he was a really silly old man,
So I shouted, "What about the Good Samaritan?"

RAT CATCHING

My friend Martin had a dog named Scrap,
Still a pup when we first showed her a rat.
She was quick and fearless, always in front,
So we decided to teach her how to hunt.

How to teach we had to stop and think,
Then we discovered she knew by instinct.
On Saturdays we went out like no others,
Becoming the Fen's 'Great White Hunters'.

We'd find a rat hole in the side of a dyke,
There was always a bolt-hole out of sight.
Needing to find it to block the escape,
Then we'd let Scrap go in the front gate.

She would dig at a truly frantic pace,
And dirt would fly all over the place.
We kept an eye on the sealed bolt-hole,
In case the rat thought it was a mole.

The excitement grew as the dog got near,
Now and then a squeak we might hear.
With a violent shake of Scrap's head,
In less than a second the rat was dead.

Often we took carbide, but not for lamp fuel.
Looking back now it all sounds quite cruel,
But it's what we grew up with back then,
That's how it was for boys living in the Fen.

GRANDAD'S TRICYCLE

When Martin moved to Barkham's Lane,
Things were never quite the same.
We still had fun and messed about,
Always good pals, without a doubt.

He now lived next to his grandad's dairy,
Where barns and fridges were customary.
I knew this man as 'Granddad Hiblin',
For many years before I knew Martin.

Clinking the bottles, you'd hear him coming,
Delivering milk when the birds start chirping.
On Friday he'd knock and come charging in,
Jingling his money with one finger missing.

As adventurers we explored his dusty barn,
Finding a tradesman's trike old and forlorn.
With a big cradle over the two front wheels,
And a big handbrake that always squeals.

We washed it down and doing our best,
Gave it some oil and ignored the rust.
The cradle held eight milk crates,
Too wide to get through most gates.

With me in the front and Martin in the saddle,
That old trike groaned as he started to pedal.
Down Hempfield Road, we hummed along,
Stopping when we reached Millpit Furlong.

Then turning back towards Barkham's Lane,
Laughing loud, people thought we were insane.
We came to the first bend at phenomenal speed,
That corrugated fence looked a menace indeed.

Martin pulled on the brake with all his might,
I hung on for dear life, with knuckles white.
But as we went through a hole in the road,
The cradle broke under the new-found load.

Dropping on the front wheels making them stick,
The trike could only go straight and that was it.
We hit that old fence with a mighty crash,
Knocking a panel out, giving another a bash.

Martin flew over my head, landing in front of me,
My feet were in the cradle and an arm in a tree.
Gathering ourselves and being unhurt,
We fell into fits of laughter from the heart.

Seeing what damage we had just done,
We grabbed the trike and started to run.
Returning the machine to Grandad's barn,
Knowing this would be our secret yarn.

For a long time Martin and I were inseparable and had many adventures. Some would have inspired Enid Blyton or Mark Twain. To quote Martin: 'We did things, that these days you would never dare let your children do alone – we were so lucky'. My friendship with Martin and our exploits remain my fondest memories. We shared a wholesome bond that every boy should experience.

MARTIN AND I

Martin was bought a two-seater canoe,
His mum said, "Two seats, one is for you."
His mum and dad didn't forget me ever,
We couldn't wait to try it out on the river,

Paddling, attempting to get in synch,
Trying not to make our paddles clink.
It didn't take long till we stroked together,
We had so much fun, in any old weather.

Inspired by our adventures in the Scouts,
We decided on another, there and abouts.
Planning to paddle to the Fish and Duck,
We'd get there in a day, with a bit of luck.

Planning and scheming about all we'd take
Was as much fun as the journey we'd make.
Deciding we'd go for more than a week,
Realising the Ouse was not just a creek.

We stowed food, sleeping bags and a tent,
And many more things before we went.
When we set off there was nobody about,
But we were happy the sun had come out.

Soon we came upon our first landmark,
Where the Ouse meets the river Lark.
We stopped for a while to adjust our stow,
It was in good shape and we had to go.

Paddling for hours made our arms ache,
So once in a while a rest we might take.
Taking turns while the other still stroked,
So not to lose time, is what we hoped.

In the distance a great building we saw,
It's where they took sugar beet, for sure.
By the wharf something went floating by,
Didn't know what, and we wondered why.

Paddling over to see what fate had sent,
We both grabbed for it and over we went.
In the water we turned the canoe upright,
Then swam to the shore in a bit of a fright.

We had heavy clothes on to keep us warm,
I started to sink, wondering will anyone mourn?
Martin was a strong swimmer, easy to see,
A great deal better than little old me.

So I called for help, before it was too late,
Men came running, calling, "Hang on, mate."
They had a boathook and said to grab hold,
Dragging us in, the water was getting cold.

Taking us away to a little brick shed,
With a big iron stove and coals all red.
Staying there until we had dried out,
Telling them what we had been about.

We dried the canoe and got ready to go,
They wanted to tell our mums, we said, "No."
But somehow folks knew about our caper,
As a piece appeared in the Littleport Paper.

Martin and I decided to go the other way,
We'd go to Stretham some other day.
Back north, past where we had already been,
Hoping to pass Littleport without being seen.

To the Ship Inn we came by late afternoon,
It was not open then, but it would be soon.
Given permission to camp by the river there,
Martin phoned his mum to say where we were.

Pitching our tent right on the water's edge,
There was a jetty making a sort of a ledge.
You can be sure we slept soundly that night,
In our little tent with the door tied up tight.

We heard the water and sounds in the dark,
Splash, squeak and a rustle, like a nature park.
Martin made breakfast, while I went to fish,
It would be my turn to create the next dish.

We explored the area for most of the day,
Paddling up the Little Ouse as far as we may.
That night there was a great thunderstorm,
We stayed in our tent and tried to keep warm.

Filling our tent to keep everything dry,
Didn't leave much room for Martin and I.
It was difficult not to touch the canvas skin,
But everywhere we did, the rain came in.

We heard a voice calling us at one o'clock,
Then on our tent pole there came a knock.
"Come in, boys, you can't stay out here."
Together in a hot bath, we found us pair.

Waking in the sheets of a nice warm bed,
Then given breakfast, we were very well fed.
Back to our adventure and dry out our things,
"Hey, last night we got no mosquito stings."

Two young girls appeared on the bridge,
Gloria lived in a house by the water's edge.
They came back later and, to our surprise,
Brought us little home-made rhubarb pies.

We promised to see them the very next day,
No interest in girls, wondering what we'd say.
Paddling along we soon found Gloria's house,
She met us on the bank, as cute as a mouse.

The house was empty but Stephanie was there,
We chatted and laughed and they gave us fare,
Then Gloria said, "Quick! My mum is coming.
No! not out the front, she will see you leaving."

Climbing through a window at the back,
We landed in a big old rhubarb patch.
Over the bank to the canoe without delay,
Then it started to rain, a bit like yesterday.

Back to the vegetables and, being on our guard,
We pulled handfuls of tops off Gloria's rhubarb.
In the canoe we covered ourselves to keep dry,
With one each on our heads we laughed till we'd cry.

These adventurous days quickly shot past,
We didn't want them to be over quite so fast.
We laid on the bank and stared at the sky,
Talking about things that money couldn't buy.

NEW SCHOOL

They sent me to the Martin School,
Just so I wouldn't grow up to be a fool.
"Nice new classrooms," said Art Teacher Ted,
When we arrived it looked more like a big shed.

"It's not finished," we all complained,
"It looks like the builder stopped when it rained."
But Mr Lister got stern and saved the day,
"Get in there, kids, you are here to stay!"

"Call Law Brothers," Winnie said,
"I'll pop home and get George out of bed."
So we went to a school with scaffold poles,
Dump trucks, and sports fields full of holes.

Now Robert Browning is a famous name,
Our Headmaster had one just the same.
If we did wrong he'd cast a scowl,
Always prepared … he'd met Baden-Powell.

A perfect gentleman through and through,
The very best example for me and you.
He was firm and didn't tolerate louts,
Oh yes, he also ran the Cubs and Scouts.

He managed that school like a gem,
I'd be quite happy to be back there again.
Now what about all the teachers there,
You only played them up if you dare.

Mr Browning taught science and chemistry,
To tell the truth it sort of … bypassed me.
We mixed things up and put them on Bunsen burners,
Talk about stink, but not as bad as our school dinners.

Mrs Morton was good, kind and fair,
Put us in a play, our mums and dads were there.
A story about lost treasure and King John,
We were really nervous when we went on.

We had a lot of fun back then,
I was dressed up as one of King John's men.
She made us learn our lines good and proper,
Daren't do anything else, her husband was a copper.

Miss Strawson, otherwise known as June,
Made her presence felt in the classroom.
She huffed and puffed trying to keep us busy,
By lesson's end her class were all quite dizzy.

Her basic geography was always a hoot,
Learning how to go home by another route.
English was fun with no glimpse of sorrow,
"If you ever get stuck just say wheelbarrow."

With Mr Cottier for maths and poetry,
That's when I spent time in purgatory.
We had a silent understanding, you see,
I didn't like him and he didn't like me.

He did things, that nowadays he wouldn't dare,
But he'd never do them with other teachers there.
He liked to jest, so laughing was not a sin,
But only if the joke had come from him.

Mrs Browning taught music and some other thing,
She had a great passion to make us sing.
Some kids learned music with great ease,
But to me it was never more than Chinese.

Being in the choir was a love–hate thing,
Kids hated her shouting, but liked to sing.
Sadly one dark day she went and died,
Taking with her the choir's tears as they cried.

We had a teacher named Mrs Dring,
But she didn't teach me anything.
That's because she never took our class,
Now I suppose I'm being a silly arse.

Mr Hughes, from teacher-training school,
Had a Welsh accent, but he was no fool.
He didn't understand much Fen, of course,
He thought 'dockey' was a man who rode a horse.

Now Mr Partridge, he was good,
Showed us how to make things out of wood.
When I think of him I have to say,
I still use what he taught me to this day.

Art with Mr Chamberlain, some called him Ted.
A tall, stern man with no hair on his head.
In the classroom he didn't like chatter or talk,
If he heard you, he was 'Dead Eye Dick' with a bit of chalk.

My form teacher, Mr Roberts, cycled there from Ely,
Taught geography and english, but preferred history really.
All about Sir Francis Drake, the Armada and how it had been,
He had a minibus and took us to places we'd never seen.

We went to Cambridge to see *Twelfth Night*,
We saw drunk Sir Toby, that was a funny sight.
Kind hearted and considerate, I'm not kidding,
He was a perfect reincarnation of Mr Chipping.

In the hall Mrs Collen strutted her stuff,
It was modern dancing for all of us.
She picked on me to dance with her,
Held me close and everything went a blur.

Miss Wilson sometimes showed her flair,
Had us country dancing in a square,
"Find your partners and do-se-do,
Or off to see Bob Browning you will go."

Religious instruction with Mrs Vail,
From the Bible she would tell a tale.
She spoke softly as we sat in front of her,
Telling stories of Gold, Frankincense and Myrrh.

To the gym for PT and games with Mr Speed,
No mucking about there, him you had to heed.
It was quite often that his anger flared,
But it was only because he really cared.

From fifty years memories are in 'retrieve',
I was fortunate to go there, I do believe.
Around the world I've been since then,
But I won't forget my school near Woodfen.

They changed its name but I don't care,
It's the same place to me, and it's still there.
I hear they're going to knock it to the ground,
But my memories will never be pulled down.

No, I won't leave my name,
That is if it's all the same.
These are just my memories you see,
And I don't want PC Morton catching up with me.

SCHOOL ANOMALIES

Taught algebra and not told why,
An apple plus an orange equals y.
With no suggestion of application,
Nothing to aid your comprehension.

Spelling being marked on just speed
At using a dictionary when you need.
Searching a dictionary to find how it's spelt,
You had to know first or you couldn't find out!

Compositions marked on neatness alone,
Didn't matter what brilliance you'd shown.
Tone-deaf and being asked to sing,
Being told to put a 'semi-quaver' in??

Chemistry formula taught parrot fashion,
Then asked to apply them all with passion.
Alas, poor Mr Cloe, for he is no more,
What he thought was H_2O was H_2S0_4.

Poetry exams just a test of memory,
No appreciation for the poet's story.
Having to remember verses by rote,
No concern for what the poet wrote.

Told not to be afraid at the school dentist,
Watching a friend carried out unconscious.
From a hole where once had been a tooth,
Red blood dripping from an open mouth.

An abstract subject to paint in a rush,
Not being shown how to use the brush.
Being told not to waste time in class,
Teachers interrupting while going past.

Hurrying to go nowhere at all,
Running on the spot like a fool.
Told Latin names you must not lose,
With nowhere they would be used.

Life was full of anomalies and woe,
Coming or going you just didn't know.
Seeing the funny side was always best,
Treating it all with a big spoonful of jest.

SWIMMING GALA

At Sandhill Bridge on the Great Ouse,
Our annual swimming gala was big news.
Full of excitement, kids practised down there,
Each determined to enter and win their share.

Changing in corrugated huts on the bank,
If someone peed in them, they really stank.
Lifting and dropping the duckboards made a racket,
Beneath were coins, fallen from anyone's pocket.

The bridge was a big, grey steel affair,
There was high diving from up there.
One year a man fell from the top board,
It had only been tied on with a bit of cord.

A strange-looking old lady along the bridge ran,
Shouting and screaming, carrying a frying pan.
The first time I saw her, I thought she was real,
It was a man dressed up, his trunks concealed.

Officials pretended to catch her on the run,
I really thought it was someone's mum.
Then in a flurry, she'd dive in with a scream,
Swimming underwater so as not to be seen.

Across the river two barges placed well apart,
We'd swim between them and back to the start.
For boys of eleven the 100 yards dash,
I was not very good but I gave it a bash.

To start we were all together on the barge,
But in the water the gap grew quite large.
When most boys had finished, I'd got halfway,
But being able to finish would make my day.

Getting out of the water I could hardly stand,
The crowd cheered, someone gave me a hand.
I won no prizes, but touched a few hearts,
And too tired to line up for any more starts.

Our annual village gala down by the bridge
Attracted a club all the way from Cambridge.
Too professional, they were not liked much,
They got all cocky winning most of the cups.

When it was finished the fun was not over yet,
Waiting to see winners in the *Littleport Gazette*.
Derek Crouch's men took the barges away,
But they would be back next year, on gala day.

SCHOOL DINNERS

Our canteen was on the other side of the yard,
Through the 'bigguns' school', it wasn't hard.
Next to the school gardens all looking green,
With students' allotments, a sight to be seen.

Our school dinners were not up to much,
Mashed potatoes that looked like slush.
With some runny bits and many a lump,
They hit the plate with a soggy thump.

Boiled cabbage several times a week,
The unhappy effect would make you reek.
Chopped beetroot was a poor replacement,
So hard you could use it on the pavement.

Lucky when you got chopped spam,
They told us kids that it was really ham.
Sometimes a piece of baked fish,
So small you didn't need a dish.

Then jelly that looked like green frog's spawn,
Or a piece of jam tart with watery custard on.
On this, we'd never grow up big and strong,
And the kitchen always let out a terrible pong.

Sitting at the table, there was a lot of chatter,
Teachers ignored us, obviously it didn't matter.
We swapped our vegetables for what we liked,
When it was over, our faces we wiped.

Before long we were hungry again,
We tried to ignore the stomach pang.
"May I go to the toilet, please?" I had an idea,
So as I asked, I tried to look very sincere.

Mr Cockerel said, "Go, and don't be long."
There was no hesitation, then I was gone.
To the allotments, where carrots and peas grew,
I knew for sure I'd find something there to chew.

With a handful of vegetables to the cycle shed,
I'd sit there for as long as it took, till I was fed.
Realising someone might easily see me,
I had to move, would it be to the lavatory?

I considered it hard, and had a think,
Deciding against it, because of the stink.
Next to the cycle shed was a big coal bunker,
It was dusty and dirty but a whole lot safer.

Closing the gate, I sat there on the coal,
All by myself, without another soul.
How long I was there I really don't know,
Never occurring that to class I had to go.

The gate opened like something sinister,
With a shovel in his hand stood Mr Lister.
He immediately took me to see Miss Davy,
So afraid, I could have pooped like gravy.

With a face covered in coal dust and dirt,
You couldn't tell the colour of my shirt.
Miss Davy got angry and barked at me,
Then caned my bum. One, two, three.

SCOUT MASTERS

When I joined the Scouts it meant a lot to me,
And I really liked our scoutmasters, all three.
It was an open troop and all were welcome,
For anyone to leave it was very seldom.

Mr Browning was the Group Scoutmaster,
He also doubled as our school headmaster.
A GSM was traditionally known as 'Skip',
But for respect at school we never let it slip.

The school caretaker was a scoutmaster as well,
Stories about the Home Guard he loved to tell.
Mr Lister had a limp, his enthusiasm it didn't stop,
And with much respect, we knew him as 'Hop'.

Mr Speed, who taught sports, games and athletics,
Became a scoutmaster, now accepting our antics.
At Scouts there were no school desks to thump,
Because of what he taught he was known as 'Jump'.

We had a unique team of dedicated gentlemen,
Such great adventures we had because of them.
They tolerated much and never got the hump,
With affection they were Hop, Skip and Jump.

SCOUT CAMP

You had to be eleven to join the Scouts,
Then you could be part of the fun thereabouts.
To belong had long been my great desire,
Since I heard they'd teach me to light a fire.

Learned knots, lashings and other things,
And all that you could do with two old strings.
Morse code and flashing torches was really a must,
Getting the message through was, **** or bust.

Our den was under the Martin School stage,
It was small and cramped, more like a cage.
Holding all our gear, it was our first real home,
Which quickly became hallowed ground to some.

Every year we went on our annual camp,
To where it rained and was usually damp.
To Broadstone Warren the whole troop went,
That was my first time at living in a tent.

We found a stick cross, was something dead?
We took our hats off and lowered our head.
It took a few days to discover what it was for,
When we moved our latrine we knew the score.

At making furniture, Mr Browning was good,
All from sticks and ferns and odd bits of wood.
We made tables and benches for our mess tent,
But when Mr Lister sat down, the whole lot bent.

Playing backwoods games like never before,
Roaming the woodlands, life was never a bore.
Rotating in turn to cook food for the troop,
Playing tricks on everyone, what a hoot.

Scoutmasters filled their tent with tobacco smoke,
To sleep in peace, making the mosquitoes choke.
Scouts played pranks and giggled all night long,
While trying to remember words to a campfire song.

We were happy to smell of old wood smoke,
And looking untidy compared to most folk.
But we'd have great memories forever more,
These are the adventures boys are made for.

When it was over nobody wanted to go home,
As we packed, some boys started to moan.
Scoutmaster said, "There is always next year."
And any one of us could have shed a small tear.

Next year eventually came, as it always does,
We were off to Kent, to Kingsdown on a bus.
As the excitement grew, I could almost explode.
Then my sister gave me chickenpox,
And I forgot the Scouting code!

BILLY SHAY'S NEW WATCH

As a Cub Scout Billy was a likeable lad,
Of note was the loud voice that he had.
Being heard above the rest of the pack,
Simply anywhere, he never held back.

On Remembrance Day Billy carried the flag,
Seeing it as an honour, one he had to have.
His wish was granted and training given,
A big job for a boy, but Billy was driven.

He'd been given a new watch to tell the time,
Showed everyone, saying proudly, "It's mine."
When the big day came he was very good,
At carrying the flag as we thought he would.

Assembling first at the Gas House Green,
Standing in straight lines, a sight to be seen.
The Cubs got in step as the band struck up,
Marching to the cenotaph without a hiccup.

Billy stood proud as the names were read,
Then quiet for a minute bowing his head.
Getting cold, he didn't think much of this,
Then to the church for the main service.

Tributes were read and the 'Last Post' heard,
Canon Payne delivered his sermon with verve.
He'd considered and calculated well beforehand,
Here for only one hour out of so many thousand.

The Canon had done his homework,
He got excited, going off like firework.
Billy got agitated and wriggled around,
Being chastised, not liking the sound.

Checked his watch, plucked up the nerve,
Calling to the Canon so everyone heard,
"We've already been here more than an hour."
Billy was annoyed and was not about to cower.

As Billy's voice echoed inside the church,
Canon Payne almost fell right off his perch.
His mouth dropped open, his face went pale,
Billy had taken the wind right out of his sail.

Agreed, the Canon preached too long,
But Billy couldn't see anything wrong.
He was firmly told to exercise refrain,
If he ever wanted to carry the flag again.

THE PERILS OF BOB-A-JOB

Washing a car too big made you grapple,
Then instead of a bob they'd give an apple.
Dig the garden and clean out the pond,
A filthy old job of which nobody was fond.

Afraid to go down the garden path,
Was the owner really a psychopath?
Going back after lunch to get your bob,
Finding a note: 'Had to go out on a job'.

Wash an old dog with terrible mange,
"Sorry, son, I don't have any change.
I'll take a sticker showing you were here,
I can't find the one I was given last year."

"Sorry, I don't have any jobs, not one,
But I'd like a sticker to say 'Job Done'."
Fetch the paper and do some shopping,
For a lady who thought it was for nothing.

Performing a job, often a difficult task,
For your bob having to repeatedly ask.
Kneeling on the lawn to pull out the weeds,
A dog on your back trying to satisfy its needs.

Clean out the shed with an old broomstick,
Working your guts out to be given a comic.
Collect the eggs and muck out the chickens,
For an old miser who would inspire Dickens.

Cleaning the windows, every pane,
You won't get paid if it starts to rain.
Cutting a wet lawn with a rusty old mower,
The grass too long, making it even slower.

Some people left jobs for far too long,
Waiting for Boy Scouts to come along.
Getting it done for almost nothing was a plus,
Trying not to let them take advantage of us.

THE DANCING LESSON

Mr Lister cleaned and polished the floor,
As was his custom the night before.
With great patience and so much time,
Making that parquet gleam and shine.

You would wonder what it was readied for,
Were dignitaries to come through the door?
But the honour was for our dancing class,
Which surely, Mrs Collen thought was a farce.

Teaching country girls some finer, formal steps,
And plodding farm boys who would never be adept.
Connie, was nice, understanding and often sweet,
She had a big smile, and a figure *oh so petite.*

Announcing that she would teach the quick-step,
She ordered us into a circle to watch her prep.
Moving as though she was floating on air,
With sensual grace she made the boys stare.

At that moment big John Cole sauntered in,
Slowly, with caution, and wearing a silly grin.
Connie said. "Where have you been, tell me?"
"Sorry Miss". He mumbled. "Had to have a pee".

"I beg your pardon! Your manners you do forget"
Big John looked down. "Sorry I went to the toilet".
Then under his breath he muttered. "For a pee".
Stifling a grin, Connie turned so we couldn't see.

An imaginary partner didn't offer much scope,
So she asked for a volunteer, without much hope.
With a mixture of desire and bashful repose,
Boys stood around until one of us she chose.

I saw her point at me as though it was surreal,
Red faced and afraid this was to be my ordeal.
Inviting me to the middle of the room with her,
Others relieved as they gave a low, sighing cheer

"First watch, then relax and follow my lead,
Don't hold your breath you're allowed to breath".
Standing at arms length as for an old fashioned waltz,
She looked at me saying. "No, we've got to get close".

Then taking me to her in the correct pose,
We stood just like statues, nose to nose.
"I want to feel your thighs touching mine,
If I can't, you will never move in time".

This really made my young heart beat,
And would surely give me two left feet.
Trying hard not catch anyone's eye,
There was no point now in being shy.

If we stand too long my knees will tremble,
Already beads of sweat running down each temple.
Her warmth went straight to my head,
Confused, I wanted to be anywhere else instead.

When the music started we were off,
Me hanging on like a doll made of cloth,
Backwards Connie shot across the room,
How I wished this would be over real soon.

All around the room we strutted, not out of puff.
I was beginning to enjoy this dancing stuff.
She eased me away saying. “What did you think?”
After my awkward smile, she gave a knowing wink.

After this class the other boys all wanted to know,
How it was in Connie’s arms, going quick-quick slow.
As I recounted with much bravado and embroidery,
For some days I was the focus of boys lustful envy.